USING HERBS IN THE HOME

USING HERBS IN THE HOME

ANTHONY GARDINER

SELECT
EDITIONS

This edition published in 1996 by
Promotional Reprint Company Ltd
Kiln House, 210 New Kings Road
London SW6 4NZ
for Selecta Book Ltd, Devizes, Wiltshire, UK

Copyright
Text © Anthony Gardiner 1995
Layout and Design © Promotional Reprint Company Ltd 1996

ISBN 1 85648 380 0

ACKNOWLEDGEMENTS

Recipes kindly supplied by:
Mary Berry (p30), Anna Del Conte (p26), Liz and Dan Fleming (pp31, 32),
Jane Gardiner (pp23, 24), Sarah Mertens (p23).

Publisher's Note

Neither the Publisher nor the Author take any responsibility for the implementation of
any recommendations, ideas or techniques expressed or described in this book. Any use
to which the recommendations, ideas and techniques are put is at the Reader's sole deci-
sion and risk.

Printed and bound in China

CONTENTS

Of Pot-Pourris and Tussie Mussies

The most common usage of herbs in the home today by far is in floral decoration. In a way this is not so far removed from the days when herbs were used to sweeten the air in smoke-filled houses that also reeked of all kinds of filth. As tastes became more refined these herbs became known as strewing or manger, herbs, suggesting their use to sweeten the straw in the baby Jesus' manger.

Traditional strewing herbs are woodruff, meadowsweet, thyme, pennyroyal, lavender, roses, violets and winter savory. Out of all of these I most love to bring woodruff into the house in the summer. Tied in bunches to hang in the kitchen it appears to have no scent at all, until it dries. Then with each passing day it gives off a heady aroma of new-mown hay that takes you right back to the country every time you walk past it.

Lavender too has a very refreshing scent. After drying, place it in open bowls so that you can dip your fingers in it as you pass by. It sweetens the air and lightens your senses too. Lavender used to be burned in a sickroom to fumigate it, and for a long time lavender bags were very fashionable – you can still find them in some craft shops to this day. But there is no reason why you should confine yourself to lavender in bags, sachets or small drawstring bags. A mixture of sweet-smelling wild flowers or various dried herbs can be used, whichever suits your nose.

The traditional nosegay was so called because it was carried close to the nose to disguise foul smells from the city drains and crowded places. A drop or two of essential oil on a tissue can have the same effect. There are some herbs that repel moths and make good fresheners at the same time. Southernwood, *Artemisia camphorata,* and camphor plant are all effective. They can either be tied up in bunches or placed in cotton bags which can then be hung as near as possible to the probable source of infestation.

Another favourite form of room freshener is pot-pourri. Endless combinations can be achieved by mixing all kinds of dried petals and leaves with a fixative – such as orris root – to preserve them. I have a simple carrier basket by the fire with a selection of scented geranium leaves and old-fashioned rose petals, which has lasted all winter long. Other suitable containers include elaborate porcelain jars and pots with perforated lids which release the scent into the room. When the fragrance of the mixture begins to fade you can add a few drops of essential oil to cheer it up.

Right: **A mass of sweet woodruff beneath a canopy of hops in the author's garden.**

Burners, or vaporisers, for essential oils have a little dish placed above a small candle to warm the oil and allow its scent to pervade a room. If you are using pure essential oil it is best to mix it with a carrier such as grapeseed oil, or a few drops of water. The use of these burners is far preferable to aerosol sprays and there is no risk to the atmosphere. Apart from all that, they do smell much better.

If you have cats, then do remember to dry some catnip (*Nepeta cataria*) and keep it in a sealed jar. Whenever you want to give them a treat, take a little of the dried herb and strew it on the carpet. They love it. You can, of course, make a small felt mouse and fill it with catnip as a toy for your pet.

Scented bookmarks can be made by drying the leaves of costmary (*Chrysanthemum balsamita*). This was known as 'Bible leaf' because it was put to this use in monasteries. The leaf, once dried, takes on a translucent quality and retains its balm-like scent for ages. It won't stain the leaves of your book either.

Herbs can and have been used for all sorts of household uses in the laundry too. At one time when housewives had sheets to dry, they often placed them over box hedges. In this way the sheets were nicely scented for the bedroom. Today bunches of woodruff and meadowsweet can be placed between the sheets of the bed after making.

Herbs were used, as they are to this day, to scent soaps for the household. They can also be used to make furniture creams and polishes. In Elizabethan times it was customary to polish furniture with bunches of lemon balm (*Melissa officinalis*). In Shakespeare's play *The Merry Wives of Windsor*, one of the characters, Anne Page, says: 'The several chairs of order look you scour/With juice of balm, and every precious flower.'

The natural oils not only brought out the shine but gently scented the furniture as well. Horsetail is rich in silica and has been used to scour saucepans; because of this it became known as 'pewterwort'. The only unfortunate thing about horsetail is its invasive nature. It is one of the most primitive plants alive today, and dates back to prehistoric times. Horsetail is therefore one of nature's great survivors.

The art of dyeing

The art of dyeing using plant material is not entirely lost - it has just been overtaken by chemical dyes. It is, however, necessary to use a chemical mordant of iron, alum, chrome or tin to make the dye permanent. The soft colours obtained from herbs quickly fade without a mordant. Yellows and brown are the simplest colours to make, but plants such as

Right: The finely toothed leaves of costmary should be picked while young as in this picture.

madder can produce quite strong oranges which are closer to being red. Quite a lot of plant material is needed, so rather than denude your garden you should buy dried materials. Even in the earliest descriptions of the dyeing process, the need for a special building is suggested. Jean Hellot in *The Art of Dyeing* (1789) says, 'Your Dye house must be spacious and lightsome, and as near as possible to a running stream, water being absolutely necessary for preparing your Woolens and for rinsing them after they are dyed.'

Dyeing is quite a smelly process and water should be close at hand. You will also need a large dye bath, preferably stainless steel, a bucket and bowl, wooden tongs, stirrers, a measuring jug, a pair of scales and rubber gloves. You need to protect your hands from the chemicals in the mordant and to avoid dyeing yourself. Jean Hellot goes on to describe using a cold vat with urine.

> 'Four pounds of Indigo powdered into a gallon of vinegar. Leave to digest over a slow fire for 24 hours. Pound in a mortar and add a little urine. Afterwards put in half a pound of madder mixing well with a stick. Pour into a cask containing 50 gallons of urine … It is of no consequence whether it be stale or fresh. Stir morning and evening for 8 days.'

I understand that in 19th century Scotland as much as 3,000gal of human urine were collected daily for the manufacture of Harris Tweed.

Wreaths, tussie mussies and herb trophies

Herbal wreaths have been popular since the time of the Romans. Simple wreaths of bay were used then to adorn the heads of heroes and champions of war; also for poets and artists. The wreath is symbolic of the holistic nature of life and represents the continual cycle and belief in immortality. You can make up scented wreaths that impart their scent as the herbs dry on them, or you can create a wreath to suit a wedding, or religious festival.

We usually associate wreaths with Christmas, but they can just as well be made to celebrate Easter or Advent. Artemisias make a good base, with rosemary and lavender to fill them out. I like to add cinnamon sticks and nutmegs tied with ribbons to winter wreaths. You can also place your wreath in a tray or bowl lined with moss to retain moisture and use it as a table decoration. All sorts of herbs that dry well can be used, and cones from evergreen trees as well as dried fruit added to your design.

Right: A tussie mussie is easy to make, although you can elaborate on the paper holder, as shown here.

Herb pillows have long been enjoyed to aid relaxation and sleep. Hop pillows have traditionally been used as sleep pillows, but you can make up any mixture of dried herbs, rather in the same way as you would make up a pot-pourri. Placed inside a lining of muslin it can then be inserted into any pillow material, for example velvet, brocade or cotton. There is no need to make the pillow very large, the scent will remain for some weeks. Herbs to use include lemon balm, thyme, hops, rosemary, southernwood, scented geraniums, lemon verbena and lavender.

Large bouquets of herbs are known as 'trophies' and smaller posies are called 'tussie mussies'. Tussie mussies originated from sweet-smelling posies carried by ladies to ward off bad smells and, reputedly, infectious germs. Trophies were given as presents and often had a symbolic significance depending on the herbs included. Rosemary indicated friendship, southernwood was a love token and symbol of good luck and sweet marjoram brought joy. To add a bit of fun you can make up a saint's trophy or one made of flowers mentioned by Shakespeare. I like to plunder the garden in mid-summer and gather as many as look beautiful into a trophy for the flower vase.

Herb recipes

Recipes for polishes and pot-pourri have been handed down from one generation to another. The introduction of housekeeping manuals in the 18th century by such women as Susanna Whatman, Elizabeth Smith and Hannah Glasse led eventually to the publication of Mrs Beeton's definitive book on household management, in 1860. Here is an interesting herb recipe for cleaning floors from Hannah Glasse's *Servant Directory* published 100 years earlier.

'Take tansy, mint and balm; first sweep the room, then strew the herbs on the floor, and with a long hard brush rub them well over the boards till you have scrubbed the floor clean. When the boards are quite dry, sweep off the greens and with a dry rubbing brush, dry rub them well, and they will look like mahogany, of a fine brown, and never want other washing. This gives a sweet smell to the room ... You may use fennel or any sweet herbs that are green, or what you can get; but tansy, mint, balm and fennel are the best herbs.'

A Victorian recipe for pot-pourri comes from *Fragrant Flowers and Leaves* by Donald McDonald (1895).

'Gather early in the day and when perfectly dry, a peck of Roses, pick off the petals and strew over them three quarters of a pound of common salt. Let them remain two or three days, and if fresh flowers are added, some more salt must be sprinkled over them. Mix with the roses half a pound of finely pounded bay salt, the same quantity of allspice, cloves and brown sugar, a quarter of a pound of gum benzoin, and two ounces of powdered orris root. Add one gill of brandy and any sort of fragrant flowers, such as orange and lemon flowers, lavender and lemon-scented verbena, and any other sweet-scented flowers. They should be perfectly dry when added. The mixture must be occasionally stirred and kept in close-covered jars, the covers to be raised only when the perfume is desired in the room. If after a time the mixture seems to dry, moisten with brandy only, as essences too soon lose their quality and injure their perfume.'

FURNITURE POLISH

Modern methods of making furniture polish and floor
polishes use beeswax, turpentine, linseed oil and soap flakes.
Here is a simple recipe from an Irish friend of mine, who
now lives in France. It is lovely and creamy and you can add
an infusion of rosemary, lavender or lemon balm to scent it:

Melt 1 (medium) candle and 75g/3⅓oz of beeswax in a small
saucepan. Add 600ml/1 pint of real turpentine. Dissolve 10½
tablespoons of soap powder (flakes) in 600ml/1 pint of
hot water and add to the mixture. It will look milky at this
stage. Put the saucepan in a basin of cold water to cool and
thicken.Put the polish into a screw-top bottle.

This appears to suggest that making pot-pourri is terribly complicat-
ed and builds up the sort of mystique that surrounds it today. In fact,
with a little imagination, enough plant and flower material, with the
addition of a fixative such as orris root – which is readily available at
health food shops and pharmacists – you can make it up very easily.
Choose your favourite flowers and leaves, dry them well in a cool airy
place and add whatever you like in the way of orange, lemon peel
and so on, and just remember to keep them in clean and airtight,
sealed jars.

Right: Even the small-
est flower arrangement
can be very effective.
This is an excellent
example of the adage
that less is more.

Pouncet boxes

Right: Flowering in June, the beautiful and delicate Apothecary Rose, *Rosa gallicia officinalis.*

Below: Delightfully dainty porcelain potpourris - baskets filled with sweet scented herbs.

In Shakespeare's play *Henry IV Part 1* Harry Percy, known as 'Hotspur', describes his meeting with a limpid royal messenger, sent to the field of battle to ascertain the number of captured prisoners. Hotspur describes the 'popinjay' as 'neat and trimly dressed', and 'perfumed like a milliner'. But, the worst of all, he carries with him a pouncet box to disguise the smell of carnage. In the 16th century the fashion grew for small boxes with perforated, or pounced, lids, which were used to carry scented herbs and snuff. They were very small and made of gold, silver, wood or, in some cases, dried paste. These were very popular with ladies, and much to Hotspur's disgust, they were also popular with fops and dandies.

Pomanders

Pomanders derived their name from the French, *pomme d'ambre*, meaning an apple of ambergris. The simplest type of pomander is made from an orange stuck with cloves. To make a pomander ball, take a firm orange and press cloves into the skin, close together until the whole orange is covered. Put into a bowl with mixed spices (cinnamon, cloves, powdered ginger and grated nutmeg) and 15ml/3 tablespoons of orris root. Turn the orange about in the mixture until you have filled in all the cracks. Leave the pomander in the bowl overnight and turn again the next day. When it has dried out you can hang it up with ribbon, threaded through with a large-eyed needle. Lemons and limes can also be used. The scent will last for weeks.

Right: A herb border in early spring shows the benefits of careful planting.

Below: The pretty flowerheads of chives are a great attraction for bees.

Pomanders, herbal weaths, pot-pourri – all these wonderfully fragrant things come into their own in the winter months when so much of the herb garden is just a memory of warm days and sweet scents. It is comforting to think that these captured scents will return again the following year, and thereby allow the cycle of fragrance to continue.

Culinary Uses

This is, probably, where most of us came in. I can still remember as a child, one of the most distinctive tastes was my mother's parsley sauce. I didn't know at the time that I was eating a nutritious herb; but I was aware of the complementary taste it gave to the fish dish. So today, fish, without parsley sauce, doesn't seem complete.

Herbs in your diet are, without a doubt, good for you. It didn't take civilised peoples too long to realise this. The health of a nation is vital to its survival; and what better way to introduce healthy living than by encouraging the use of natural herbs to strengthen the whole system.

It is well accepted that garlic is good for the blood and, as a result, acts as a heart tonic. Herbs supplement essential vitamins, balancing the diet by a natural selection process through the taste buds. The sheer joy of eating is in the taste. Of all the senses that come into play during eating, it is the taste that makes it a pleasurable experience. Certain herbs become synonymous with certain foods – basil with tomatoes, dill or parsley with fish, rosemary with roast lamb – and we all have our own favourites. In the hands of an expert, good food can be elevated into something sensational through the clever use of herbs. Herbs are indeed as the Emperor Charlemagne once suggested, 'the praise of cooks'.

However, when using herbs for cooking it is important to remember that overkill can often ruin your food. There is no need to lavish great amounts of herbs into your dishes in the misguided belief that because they are complementary, large amounts are more beneficial. As in most other things, with the use of herbs moderation is the key to success. A dish can be ruined by the addition of a whole handful, where two leaves would have been perfect.

The recipes included here are all tried and tested by myself and some very good friends, including one or two expert cooks. While enjoying them I hope that, like me, you will realise how lucky we are to be spoilt by nature's bounty.

Right: **Sorrel and lettuce soup with chervil.**

Soups

GARLIC OR ONION POTAGE

From Thomas Tryon's *The Good Housewife* (1692)

Take water and oatmeal, stir it together and when it is ready to boyle bruise as much garlick or onion as you please, to make it either strong or weak, put this bruised garlick into your boyling hot gruel and brew it to and fro with your ladle that it may not boyl, for five or six minutes; then take it off and let it stand a little, then add butter, salt and bread and eat it as warm as your blood. 'Tis a brave, warm, cleansing Gruel, nothing so strong and nauseous as that which is boyled for this way you do extract the finer and purer parts of the garlic, and leaves the strong nauseous qualities behind, but on the contrary much boyling, or boyling according to custom, does destroy the good cleansing vertues and awakens the Evil.

SOUPE DE SANTE, FOR FISH DAYS

From *The Receipt Book of Joseph Cooper*, 1654. Cooper was cook to Charles I

Take Celery, Endive, Sorrel, a little Chervil and Cabbage-lettuce well picked and washed, mince them down with a knife, squeeze the water from them, put them into a saucepan. Toss them up in Butter with a little Onion, take off all the fat, then put to them a little water from boiled Peas, and let them boil till they are tender; then put in half-a-spoonful of flour and keep moving it till it is brown. Then put in some good Fish-broth and a glass of wine, season it with Salt, Pepper, an Onion stuck with cloves, shred Parsley and a faggot of savoury Herbs, lay in the middle of your Soop-dish a French Roll fried having taken the crumb out at the bottom, cover the bottom of your dish with the crust of French Rolls, set it over a chafing dish of coals, lay the Herbs upon them and then pour the soop upon your crusts and herbs, let it stand a while to simmer, and soak the Bread. Garnish it with Turnips and Carrots and serve it up hot.

SORREL AND LETTUCE SOUP WITH CHERVIL
Serves 4

1 or 2 handfuls fresh, young sorrel leaves
1 head of lettuce
50g/2oz streaky bacon
½ tbsp chervil
900 ml/1½ pints/3¾ cups good chicken stock (not from a cube)
salt and freshly-ground black pepper, to taste

METHOD
1 Wash the sorrel and cut into fine strips. Wash and shred the lettuce.

2 Cook the bacon very gently until the fat melts; then remove the bacon pieces.

3 Cook the sorrel, lettuce and chervil (leave some for garnishing) in the remaining bacon fat until wilted. Add chicken stock and simmer gently.

4 Add seasoning to taste and garnish with the extra chervil.

MINTED PEA SOUP
Serves 4

2 x 400g/14oz tins of petit pois
200ml/1 pint/ 2 ½ cups chicken or vegetable stock
3 handfuls of chopped mint
1 tsp castor sugar
salt and freshly-ground black pepper to taste
single cream and chopped mint, to garnish

METHOD
1 Liquidise the peas in a blender or food processor. Pour into a saucepan and add the stock, sugar, mint and seasoning. Use less stock if a thick soup is preferred.

2 Simmer for 8-10 minutes. Pour into warmed soup bowls, swirl a little cream into each bowl and sprinkle with chopped mint.

This soup can also be served chilled.

Salads

SALAD OF HERBS AND LEAVES
Serves 6-8

1 lollo rosso or salad bowl lettuce
1 handful broad-leaf sorrel (pick only fresh young shoots)
1 handful buckler-leaf sorrel (pick only fresh young shoots)
1 handful salad burnet, stripped from its stalks
1 handful rocket, stripped from its stalks
a few sprigs of mint (ginger mint gives extra colour and piquancy),
lemon balm, tarragon, good king henry, lemon or orange thyme,
chives, garlic, chervil and fennel

METHOD
1 Line the bowl with the lettuce leaves.

2 Toss the other ingredients and pile into the centre.

3 Dress with a light vinaigrette and decorate with marigold petals and nasturtium flowers.

Right: The best summer salads are made with home-grown lettuce.

Far right: A tangy summer salad of mixed herbs and leaves.

Eggs

SALVIATA – SAGE OMELETTE

6 free-range eggs (size 3)
1 level tbsp flour
2 tbsp whole milk
1 level tbsp fresh sage, chopped
1 small garlic cove, finely chopped
50g/2oz/½ cup parmesan cheese, freshly grated
½ tsp salt
freshly ground black pepper, to season
1½ tbsp olive oil

METHOD

1 Lightly beat the eggs with a fork. Mix together the flour and milk and then beat into the eggs.

2 Add the sage, garlic, parmesan (save some for garnishing), salt and pepper.

3 Heat the oil in a large non-stick frying pan and then pour in the egg mixture. Turn the heat down immediately and let the mixture cook very gently.

Right: The simplest and best of ingredients, fresh herbs and free-range eggs, for creating an elegant omlette.

4 When it has nearly all set, but still shows a pool of uncooked eggs on the top, place it under a low grill until the top is set. Turn it out and serve hot, warm or cold, sprinkled with the extra parmesan.

Fish

PINK TROUT FILLETS WITH DILL AND LIME
Serves 4

50g/2oz/4 tbsp butter
grated rind and juice of one lime
4 pink trout fillets
2 tbsp dry vermouth (optional)
black pepper, to season

GARNISH:
1 lime
a handful of fresh dill

METHOD

1 Melt the butter in a wide shallow frying pan. Add the juice of one lime. Lay the trout fillets in the pan, skin side down, and cook gently until tender. This does not take long.

2 Remove the trout fillets and place on a warm serving plate.

3 Add to the pan juices the grated lime rind, vermouth and black pepper to season.

4 Pour the juices over the trout fillets and garnish with fronds of dill and lime wedges.

Right: The recipe for pink trout fillets can be easily adapted for cooking a whole trout.

Note: You may use coriander instead of dill, but I think this takes away from the delicate flavour of the trout.

Poultry

CHICKEN BREASTS STUFFED WITH SPINACH AND GREEN HERBS
Serves 6 as a main course or 10 if serving cold as part of a buffet
or picnic.

good knob of butter
large onion, chopped
1 handful fresh spinach, chopped or 225g/8oz packet frozen leaf
*   spinach, thawed and well drained, then chopped*
225g/8oz full-fat cream cheese
1 tbsp chopped herbs to include some of : thyme, savory, marjoram,
*   parsley, chives,basil and chervil*
1 egg yolk
pinch of grated nutmeg
salt and ground pepper, to season
6 boned chicken breasts (skin on)

METHOD
1 Preheat the oven to 220°C/425°F/Gas 7.

2 Melt the butter in a small pan and sauté the onion for 10 minutes
until tender. Toss in the spinach.

3 Turn into a bowl with all other ingredients except the chicken
breasts. Mix well and season with salt and pepper.

4 Place the breasts on a board, skin uppermost. Loosen the skin from
one side. Stuff one-sixth of the mixture into this pocket and replace the
skin. Do the same with the other five breasts.

5 Carefully lift each stuffed breast into a small roasting tin and brush
with butter. Roast for about 30 minutes until just done.

6 Serve hot, warm or cold cut in diagonal slices. If serving hot strain
off any juices in the tin and make a good, thin gravy, adding a little
reduced white wine and cream if liked.

Note: Take care not to overcook, or the chicken will lose its moisture
and flavour, and the bright green spinach and herbs will fade.

ROAST CHICKEN WITH FRESH TARRAGON STUFFING
Serves 4

1 large chicken (preferably free-range)
sea salt and freshly milled black pepper
1 handful fresh tarragon
2 cups freshly-made chicken stock
2 medium-sized onions
2-3 spring onions
2 tbsp tarragon vinegar
150g/6oz/3 cups freshly-made breadcrumbs
salt and pepper, to season

METHOD

1 Preheat the oven to 220°C/425°F/Gas mark 7.

2 Place the chicken upside down in a roasting pan containing about 450ml/¾ pint/1 ⅞ cups of water. (This prevents the breast drying out during cooking and enables plenty of chicken juice to be gathered for gravy at the end of the cooking period.) Season with sea salt and plenty of freshly milled black pepper, and scatter some of the fresh tarragon over the bird before roasting in the oven for about 1 hour.

3 To make the stuffing, roughly chop the onions and spring onions and, together with the tarragon vinegar, add these to the breadcrumbs. Season and add the rest of the tarragon leaves to the mixture.

4 Put this into a saucepan containing the chicken stock. Stir well over a low heat, but do not allow to brown.

5 Remove the chicken from the oven after one hour and divide.

6 Place stuffing mixture over the bottom of an ovenproof dish, arrange the chicken portions on top, baste with some of the chicken juices, and return to the oven for 10-15 minutes.

Meat

CASSEROLE OF SPRING LAMB WITH FRESH THYME
Serves 6-8

900g/2lb lamb fillet, diced
plain flour, to coat fillets
salt and black pepper, to season
1 dozen shallots
6-8 new season carrots
4 French baby turnips (skins on)
1.2L/2 pints/5 cups meat stock
bouquet garni
few sprigs of fresh thyme
1 handful tiny new potatoes, scrubbed, not peeled

METHOD
1 Preheat the oven to 180°C/350°F/Gas mark 4.

2 Seal the lamb, lightly coated in plain flour, in an ovenproof casserole over a high heat, adding salt and black pepper.

3 Add to the meat the shallots, prepared carrots and turnips. Heat the meat stock and pour over the meat and vegetables, then add sprigs of the bouquet garni and fresh thyme, saving some for garnishing the finished dish.

4 Bring back to the boil. Put the lid on the casserole and place in the oven for 1½-2 hours.

5 About 30 minutes before the end of the cooking time, add new potatoes and adjust the seasoning.

6 Serve direct from the casserole dish, garnishing with more sprigs of fresh thyme.

Sauces

FENNEL AND GOOSEBERRY SAUCE
From *The Receipt Book of Henry Howard*, 1710. Henry Howard
was cook to the Duke of Ormond

Brown some Butter in a saucepan with a pinch of flour, then put in a
few chives shred small, add a little Irish broth to moisten it, season with
salt and pepper; make these boil, then put in two or three sprigs of fennel and some gooseberries. Let everything simmer together till the
gooseberries are lovely and soft.

Below: Fennel is a very useful culinary herb. Add the seeds to vegetables and use its leaves finely chopped in soups.

LEMON KETCHUP
A 1940s war-time recipe

Mix 1 tbsp of grated horseradish with the grated rind of 6 lemons, add 2 tbsp of salt, 1 dessertspoonful each of white mustard seed and celery seed, a little mace, 6 cloves and a pinch of red pepper. Boil for 1 hour, bottle and seal while hot.

A SAUCE FOR A ROASTED RABBIT USED BY HENRY VIII
From *The Treasurie of Hidden Secrets and Commodious Conceits* by John Partridge (1586)

Take a handfull of washed Parsley, mince it small, boyle it with butter and verjuice upon a chafing dish, season it with sugar and a little pepper grosse beaten; when ready put in a fewe crummes of white bread amongst the other: let it boyle againe till it be thicke, then laye it in a platter, like the breadth of three fingers, laye of each side one rosted conny (rabbit) and so serve them.

PARSLEY SAUCE

25g/1oz/2 tbsp butter
30g/1oz/¼ cup plain flour
600ml/1 pint/2 ½ cups milk
salt and pepper, to taste
1 handful parsley, finely chopped

METHOD
1 Melt the butter in a saucepan. Remove from heat, add the flour and stir in with a wooden spoon, until you have a roux.

2 Add all the milk and the salt and pepper to taste. Return to the heat and stir continuously until the sauce boils. Then add your finely chopped parsley and stir in.

This is a pouring sauce. For a coating sauce use 50g/ 2oz/4 tbsp of butter and 60g/2oz/½ cup of flour.

TRADITIONAL MINT SAUCE

1 tsp sugar
25g/1oz/2-3 tbsp mint, finely chopped
30ml/2 tbsp boiling water
vinegar, to taste

METHOD
1 Put a small teaspoon of sugar with the finely chopped mint. Add boiling water and stir in well.

2 Leave until cold. Then add vinegar, to suit your taste.

Dessert

PINK GRAPEFRUIT AND MINT SORBET WITH GIN
Serves 6

2 x 460g/16oz tins pink grapefruit segments
75g/3oz/6 tbsp granulated sugar
100ml/4fl oz/½ cup gin
1 handful of mint, finely chopped

METHOD
1 Empty juice from both grapefruit tins into a saucepan. Add sugar and boil for 5 minutes until a syrup forms. Cool.

2 Add the grapefruit segments and gin and then liquidize. Add the finely chopped mint.

3 Put the sorbet in the deep freezer for 1 hour. Remove and stir thoroughly, then put it back into the freezer.

4 Remove from freezer and soften in the refrigerator for an hour before it is needed.

Drinks

BALM WINE

From *The Receipt Book of Richard Briggs* (1788), cook at The Globe
Tavern, Fleet Street and the Temple Coffee House

'Take twenty pounds of lump sugar and four gallons and a half of
water, boil it gently for one hour, and put it into a tub to cool; take two
pounds of the tops of green balm, and bruise them, put them into a barrel with a little new yeast, and when the liquor is nearly cold pour it on
the balm; stir it well together and let it stand twenty four hours, stirring
it often; then bung it tight, and the longer you keep it the better it will
be.'

BIRCH WINE

From E Smith's *The Complete Housewife* (1736)

The season for procuring the liquors from the birch trees is the begin-
ning of March, while the sap is rising, and before the leaves shoot
out; for when the sap is come forward and the leaves appear the
juice, by being long digested in the bark, grows thick and coloured,
which before is thin and clear.

The method of procuring the juice is by boring holes in the body of
the tree, and putting in fossets, which are commonly made of the
branches of elder, the pith being taken out. You may, without hurting
the tree, if large, tap it in several places, four or five at a time; and by
that means save from a good many trees several gallons every day. If
you have not enough in one day, the bottles in which it drops, must be
cork'd close, and rosined or waxed; however, make use of it as soon
as you can. Take the sap and boil it as long as any scum rises, skimming it all the time, to every gallon of liquor put four pounds of good
sugar, and the thin peel of a lemon; boil it afterwards half an hour,
skimming it very well; pour it into a clean tub, and when it is almost
cold, set it to work with yeast spread upon a toast. Let it stand five or
six days, stirring it often, then take such a cask as will hold the liquor;
fire a large match dipped in brimstone and throw it into the cask, stop
it close till the match is extinguished; tun your wine, and lay the bung
on light till you find it has done the working; stop it close and keep it
three months. Then bottle it off.

Right: **Pink grapefruit
and mint sorbet with
gin.**

MINT JULEP
A traditional American recipe
Serves 1

4 sprigs of mint
1 lump of sugar
1 tbsp water
50ml/2oz/¼ cup bourbon whiskey
crushed ice

METHOD
1 Muddle the mint, sugar and water in a tall glass. Fill with ice. Add bourbon but do not stir. Decorate with fresh mint sprig.

MAY WINE
A traditional German recipe

Pour a bottle of good German hock or riesling into a large bowl. Add thin slices of oranges and lemons, one glass of sherry, and sugar to sweeten to your taste. Take spring flowering stems of sweet woodruff, about one dozen. Leave to steep for at least one hour and serve into glasses.

Sometimes other scented spring flowers are floated on top with leaves of lemon balm or lemon verbena and lemon mint might be added. If preferred it may be chilled by adding ice cubes.

ELDERFLOWER CHAMPAGNE
A traditional English recipe

1 lemon
6 newly opened flowers (picked dry, before noon)
2 tbsp cider vinegar
675g/1 ½ lb/3 ⅜ cups granulated sugar

METHOD
1 Pare rind from the lemon and squeeze the juice, add to flower heads, vinegar and sugar in a large pan. Cover contents with water and stir to dissolve the sugar.

2 Cover and leave to steep for two days. Strain off and pour into glass bottles with screw top lids. Store on their sides for 2-3 weeks depending on the sparkle.

3 Serve cold with a slice of lemon. It is ready for immediate consumption and should not be stored longer than a month.

Note: Since a European Union ruling in Brussels, companies outside France are unable to name their products 'champagne'. This, however, doesn't prevent you calling your homemade drink by the traditional title of 'Elderflower champagne'.

ELDERFLOWER SYRUP
A traditional English recipe

Take a large jug and fill it with elderflower heads and cover with non-carbonated spring water. Leave overnight in a warm room. Strain off the liquid and add more flower heads. Two hours later strain again and add fresh flower heads. After a further two hours, strain and pour into a large saucepan and add 900g/2lb/4 ½ cups of sugar to each 600ml/1 pint/2 ½ cups of liquid. Warm over a gentle heat and stir until the sugar is dissolved. You may, if you wish, add the grated rind of two lemons. Allow to cool and bottle.

This is a concentrated mixture and must be diluted for a most refreshing summer drink. Carbonated water really peps it up. You could try making this recipe with lemon balm or lemon verbena.

Above: Woodruff is a traditional strewing herb giving the sweet smell of new-mown hay.

Teas and Tisanes

Herb teas originated from the French *tisane*. A tisane is looked upon as a herbal remedy for minor complaints of the digestion, a common cold or insomnia. Tisanes are aromatic; a Frenchman sees no reason why he should take a medicine that is not palatable, so the idea of a refreshing herb tea, which has the added bonus of balancing the system as well, soon became popular in other parts of Europe, and spread from there. Meadowsweet (for acid stomachs), rosemary (to invigorate) and chamomile (to help you sleep) are favourites; I take all of these. You can also make a blend from three herbs; for example, yarrow, peppermint and elderflower are a good combination for 'flu and colds. I try a mixture of St John's wort, lemon balm and chamomile for sleeplessness; and meadowsweet, chamomile and peppermint as a digestive aid.

Herb teas suit individual tastes and, while one may work for someone else, it may not necessarily work for you. Get to know the herbs you like and research them well before taking them. Most aromatics are quite safe, but you should never take any herbal tea for a prolonged period of time. If you are taking the tea as a medicine and the symptoms do not show any sign of improving after three or four days, then stop taking the tea and try another one. Equally, if you show signs of improvement and feel a bit better, then stop taking the tea and allow your body to continue the healing process.

If you wish you can use the tea as part of a study of chosen herbs, examining constituents, virtues, habit and so on. By infusing the herb you can experience where the warmth of the drink seems to go and what beneficial effects you feel from taking it. This will help to build up an overall picture of the herb and increase your understanding of the whole plant.

Making a herbal tea

If using dried herbs, measure out 5ml/1 teaspoon per person and place in a teapot or other covered container. If you are using fresh herbs then double these amounts. Pour boiling water over the leaves and flowers and allow to stand for 5-10 minutes. Strain off and drink. You may wish to add honey to sweeten the taste. Do not be tempted to put more than you need in the teapot, it will make the tea too strong. By experimenting, you will find the right proportion to suit your taste. Not all teas appeal to all people; if you don't like it, don't drink it.

Right: A peppermint tisane, preferably made from freshly picked leaves, helps in the relief of colic, nausea and flatulence.

For heartburn, make a chamomile tea as directed above. Keep it covered in a teapot, or cover the cup while infusing. An anti-spasmodic can be made from ginger root. Boil the root for 4-5 minutes and add cinnamon to taste. This is good for stomach cramps and travel sickness.

Basil is good for nausea, as is marjoram, which is also very often recommended for flatulence and asthma. For headache, you can try lavender flowers or lemon balm.

Digestive tonics

Bitter herbs are used as digestive tonics. Tonics strengthen and stimulate the digestive system and the liver. In Italy it is the custom to take a half glass of bitter herbs before a meal. These carminative herbs signal a warning to the stomach that a meal is on the way, and calm the active digestive juices.

A Recipe for a Digestive Tonic

4 sprigs of rosemary
a bunch of thyme
6 sprigs of marjoram
10 chamomile flowers
4 leaves of rue
⅓ cinnamon stick
6 cloves
red wine

METHOD

1 Place the fresh herbs and flowers in a large, wide-necked jar. Add the piece of cinnamon stick and the cloves. Pour the red wine over the ingredients sufficient to cover and fill the jar.

2 Seal the jar and store in a cool dark place for two weeks, turning occasionally. Strain off the wine and then bottle.

3 To use, take ½ glass in the evening, half an hour before your meal.

Right: Digestive tonics are made by infusing herbs in wine. Popular herbs for such tonics include thyme, marjoram, chamomile and rosemary.

Drying

Thomas Hyll, in *The Proffitable Arte of Gardening* (1568), wrote: 'And nowe those herbes (for the use of medicine) oughte to be gathered, and cut up, when as they be in a manner come, unto their full growthe, and that before the coloure of the flowers beginne to chaunge, and the seedes somewhat appeare. And this also oughte to be done, in a cleare and warm daye, and that they have been moystened with some showers fallinge two or three days before, so that they ought not to be gathered when any raine moisture, or wet dewe is on them, nor being then drie parched with the heate of the Sunne, nor in a raynie, and cloudie daie: for any of these do hynder the keaping any tyme in their virtue. Also they ought to be gathered when they be full of juice and freshe, and that not the smaller or bigger are to be chosen, but the meaner, and suche besides whiche fall not to whythering. And onely the tender toppes, the leaves, the flowers, are to be gathered and dried in the shadowe, in a place open towarde the Southe, not being moyste, and defended from the duste, and smoke, and for the better defending and preserving of them, to be putte up in bagges close bounde at the mouthe, and in boxes for that use.'

Nothing changes much in the world of gardening, except spelling perhaps. Thomas Hyll's advice on drying and harvesting have as much relevance today as they did four hundred years ago. The rules are still simple. Always harvest on a dry day, preferably with at least two dry days beforehand. Do not pick until after the dew has dried on the leaves, and before the sun has warmed the plants too much. Always choose the best looking herbs, just before flowering, in the case of culinary herbs; or, if you want flowers, before they begin to go to seed. Above all, dry your herbs in an airy place away from sunlight. So much of this advice seems commonsense, but it is so easy to forget, in the excitement of the moment, and then wonder why your jars contain grey dust instead of crisp dry leaves.

Methods of drying

Drying needs to be done as quickly as possible if the herbs are going to retain their quality. In some cases, as with artemisias or soft shrubby plants, you can tie them in loose bunches and hang them in a shady attic, or shed, as long as they have plenty of ventilation. Drying this way should take only one or two days. In the case of mints, lemon balm and soft-leafed herbs such as basil, then it helps to use an oven

Right: To dry herbs naturally, tie them up in small bunches and hang them upside down in a dry and shady room.

Above: Always collect the freshest, most perfect leaves for drying.

Right: The flowers of Golden hops can be used as a gentle sedative

on a low heat, keeping the door open. Alternatively, you can even use the microwave. I don't possess a microwave oven so I can't really recommend it personally, but I am told it can be quite effective. Place the leaves and shoots on a light baking tray with greaseproof paper under them, or on a cake rack, allowing air to circulate all around. Using an oven needs vigilance, as the time taken is quite swift compared to more natural methods.

If you are good at DIY you can make your own drying cupboard with tiered racks covered in stretched muslin or fine netting. If you have a shed you can develop this idea on a grander scale with shelves all around the walls, and an electric heater or small stove to assist the process. However, do not forget the vital ventilation.

You may be tempted to dry your herbs in bunches in the kitchen. This gives a very pretty, decorative effect, but you will never lose all the moisture. The herbs also attract grease and dust, therefore they should not be stored in jars or containers as they will quickly disintegrate and go mouldy.

Methods of storing

As soon as the herbs are dry, place them in dry bottles or screw-top jars. Always keep them in a shady place, completely away from direct light. Should you see any signs of moisture appearing, then you must

remove the leaves immediately and thoroughly dry them again before replacing in a clean, dry jar.

Other ways of storing herbs include freezing and preserving in oil. Freezing works very well for basil and parsley. For many herbs, however, the freezing process seems to take away their vital flavour and reduces them to limp blandness when they are defrosted. Place the basil leaves directly into a small carton. There is no need to wash if you have grown your herbs organically, or to cut up the leaves. Seal the lid and place in the freezer. When you need a leaf, just remove and crumble into your dish without defrosting. Parsley also retains its flavour using this method.

The flowers of borage can be preserved by placing then in an ice cube tray and filling the compartments with water, then freezing. Not only do they preserve very well, but they also look extremely decorative when added to drinks.

To preserve herbs in olive oil, always use the virgin first pressings. The light green colour gives a very pleasing effect. Make sure the leaves you use are completely dry after washing them as otherwise mould can develop later on.

Right: Tarragon, basil and aromatic bitter herbs preserved in vinegar and olive oil. 'Top up the oil as you use it to keep the herbs constantly covered.'

Below: Chives die down completely in the winter only to re-emerge in the spring, while woody-stemmed plants like thyme are evergreen and remain all year round.

Cosmetic Uses

Homemade herbal preparations for hair, nails, eyes, skin and body present a purely natural alternative to the mass produced products so expensively packaged today. They also give you the added satisfaction of knowing that whatever you use, no animals have suffered in the preparation of your lotion, oil and so on. Of course, you will have to devote a certain amount of time and effort to make your herbal cosmetics, but many of them can be bottled or put in jars to keep. Some require infusions, which in fact only takes about as much time as it does to make a cup of tea.

Once you begin to use them, consider the inner self as well. Diet can be a strong contributory factor in having a good clear complexion, and fingernails are a good indicator of health. Look after the inner body and the outer body is likely to be more attractive. Avoid chemically based beauty products and your skin can behave naturally. Spots are often a sign of toxins in the system. Start by attacking from within, to expel those harmful poisons in the blood stream; then the skin lotion, when applied, can work more effectively. If you consult a medical herbalist you will certainly be asked to give some idea of what you have eaten over the past week; the herbalist can then investigate your diet and adapt it accordingly to improve your outer appearance. The idea is to promote moderation – moderation in all things applies as much to eating and drinking as any other pursuit.

It is worth noting here that not all herbs react well on the skin. Some people will have allergic reactions to certain plants, and it is as well to carry out a 'patch-test' with the herb if you are in any doubt about this. Apply a small amount of lotion, or oil, to your skin and cover with a plaster (or lint with bandage if you are allergic to sticking plaster). After a suitable period of time, ideally 24 hours, check to see if your skin shows any signs of a reaction. The skin may be sore or angry looking. In the case of allergic reactions, stop using the substance immediately and, if necessary, seek professional advice as soon as possible. Do not continue to treat it yourself.

You do not need any special equipment to make these preparations but it is advisable to use clean pans and utensils. A measuring jug and a set of scales are useful items; glass containers can be old, but be sure to sterilise them before use. When making ointments always have the jars ready to hand so you can transfer the preparation before it begins to set. Finally, please avoid using old aluminium pots and saucepans: they can taint your cosmetics.

Herbal shampoos and conditioners

The aptly named soapwort (*Saponaria officinalis*) is an ideal base for herbal shampoos. The leaves produce a natural lather and can be made into a strong infusion, then left to simmer for five minutes.

For dark hair, use a mixture of rosemary and sage in an equally strong infusion – a good handful of herbs to 250ml/¼ pint of water. Allow to cool and add to the soapwort infusion at a ratio of three parts soapwort to one part herbal infusion. For fair hair, use chamomile and yarrow. After washing, use a herbal rinse made from a previously pre-pared infusion of any of the above herbs, or one made from nettle, parsley, burdock root (a decoction in this case) or southernwood.

For men's beards, the application of essential oils such as basil, sage or rosemary added to a base oil (grapeseed or olive oil) and brushed into the beard after washing helps to keep it healthy looking and helps to retain its sheen.

A tip for women with fair facial hair: apply the juice of a lemon to gently bleach it away.

Above: The soft colours of herbal preparations indicate the gentle quality of their restoring properties.

Preparations for nails and hands

The condition of our nails can often be a guide to our general health, and, as with general appearance, diet is an important factor in nail care. Eat plenty of protein – fish, pulses, nuts, dairy products and fresh fruit. Brewer's yeast can often supplement your diet, and herbs which are rich in silica, such as horsetail, can be taken as a tea. Use a block of beeswax to massage the nails, or almond oil if you prefer. For a nail bath, in which you soak your nails, make a strong infusion of horsetail, strain and allow to cool before using.

We are more aware of our hands than of any other part of our body. After all the work that is expected of them it is no wonder that they can become sore, cracked and ingrained with dirt. A simple way to remove dirt from under the nails is to make a paste of sugar and a little washing-up liquid. Add a little water to the paste and then work well into the nails by rubbing your hands together. Rinse in warm water and dry carefully and thoroughly.

This is an 18th century recipe for a paste for cleansing dirty hands that you might like to try.

'Take 100g/4oz of blanched almonds, beaten fine, into a quart [editor's note: 900ml/ 2 pints] of milk. As soon as it begins to boil, take it off, and thicken it with a couple of Yolks of Eggs. Set it on the fire again, let it be continually stirring both before and after the eggs are put in. When you take it off the fire, add two more spoonfuls of Oil, and put in up in a Gallipot [author's note: an earthenware pot from the Mediterranean] for use. A bit of this about the Bigness of a Walnut rubbed about the hands, the dirt will rub off, and it will render them very soft and smooth.

When you have used it, it will be proper to put on gloves. If one Person only be to use, half the quantity may suffice to be made at once, for it will not hold good above a Week.'

Personally, I have two favourite herbs for making into hand creams. They are rosemary and marigold (*Calendula officinalis*).

Herbal preparations for the eyes

Eye washes are considered to be the most soothing form of treatment for tired and sore eyes. But do be careful: do not make too strong an infusion, or depend on one treatment for too long. If you have more than just occasional soreness, you must consult either an optician or your doctor. Rue, in spite of its affect on the skin, was a good eye strengthener. With recent research disclosing that rue has a phototoxic effect, it would be very unwise to use an infusion on your eyes, as exposure to the sun could then have devastating results.

Safe eye tonics are: elderflower, eyebright (*Euphrasia officinalis*) and clary sage. For sore eyes you can use a weak infusion of yarrow or chamomile. For styes try tansy, or rub onion juice on the area very carefully. Tea bags, cucumber and even potato peel can be used as pads on the eyelids while lying down in a shady room. These will soothe and clear tired eyes. For a more herbal remedy, you can moisten cotton wool pads with witch hazel.

Herbal preparations for the skin

If, like Lady Wishfort in Congreve's play *The Way of the World*, you look like 'an old peeled wall', then at least be glad you don't feel the need to cover it with the sort of drastic action advocated in the 16th century. Our skin needs to be cleansed and fed, not poisoned and bleached. The use of mercury in the form of mercuric sulphide and soliman, as well as white lead, turned many a face, including Elizabeth I's, into a ravaged, pitted mess. Thankfully, herbal preparations have become widely used, and more sinister chemical applications outlawed. There are now numerous creams, oils, and other herbal products available . Here is an old recipe for cucumber lotion.

'Half a peck [editor's note: about 9 litres/8 quarts dry] of quince blossoms put in a pan, covered with cold water and simmered gently for an hour. Cut two large cucumbers into very thin slices and then chop finely. Put into the saucepan with the quince blossom water and boil for five minutes. Stain through muslin, and, when quite cold pour into bottles and tie down. To use, smear the lotion on the face and leave for at least ten minutes before washing.'

Herbs for normal skin are sage, peppermint, lady's mantle (*Alchemilla vulgaris*), fennel and juniper. For oily skin use chamomile, yarrow or parsley in a strong infusion mixed with egg white or buttermilk to make a face pack. Try oatmeal or yogurt to help clean out the pores. For dry skin use comfrey, salad burnet, marigold and borage. There are books devoted entirely to cosmetic herb preparations; by experimenting with various recipes you will soon discover the herbs that suit you .

Growing Herbs for Domestic Use

Herbs may be easy to grow, but because of their unruly nature and ability to grow on quickly, they need a good deal of attention. There is no such thing as a low-maintenance garden where herbs are concerned. With the ever-increasing pace of people's lives, both at home and at work, too many people are looking for an easy time out in the garden. We have come to expect a tidy, attractive environment that needs little more than a quick dust and hoover in order to get on with the serious business of leisure. All I can say is, if you want a low-maintenance garden then concrete the yard and stand a couple of ornaments about. Herb gardens are definitely not an easy option. They are living, breathing, developing things with the same sort of needs and care that is extended to any living, breathing, developing creature.

Herbs need cosseting in their infancy, feeding regularly until old enough to leave home, and a safe, secure, healthy environment in which to grow and prosper. Once you have planted them out in your garden, then comes the task of keeping them healthy and administering to their needs. Certain woody-stemmed plants need little more than a light prune each spring. Others, however, need harvesting on a regular basis to keep them healthy.

All herbs are 'useful' plants and need to be used. A large number, admittedly, have a built-in immune system and seem to avoid being infected by aphids or caterpillars. Other, softer herbs such as fennel require constant vigilance. Very often the first sign of ants climbing the stalks of plants such as angelica indicates the presence of aphids, insect pests which ants 'farm' for their milk.

Pruning, clipping, feeding, mulching and pest control apply to herbs just as much as to other plants. A simple regime from season to season with regular use and tender loving care can keep your herb garden looking fresh and healthy, and give the appearance of being natural and maintenance free. Taming herbs is always rewarding.

Pruning and clipping

The grazing habits of the wild goats found around the Mediterranean give rise to my theory that if you clip herbs lightly as if you were a wild animal foraging, then the plants recover and flourish. A fanciful theory maybe, but there is no doubt that judicial clipping and pruning is particularly beneficial to woody stemmed plants such as thyme, wall germander, box and marjoram.

Right: Herbs grow particularly well with the added protection of a brick wall - as well as looking aesthetically very pleasing against such a good backdrop.

Early pruning is essential to establish new growth and to create the right shape. Southernwood, wormwood, rue and sage all need to be cut hard back in the spring, hyssop a little later and lavender last of all. Some people prefer to clip lavender in the autumn, but I prefer to let it overwinter before lightly shaping it.

Most plants have an optimum height and object to being kept too low. It is as well to check what this is if you want a dwarf variety, so you don't end up buying lavenders that spread up to a metre wide and you can't understand why they don't respond to hard cutting back. Rosemary can be harvested in moderation for most of the year, but it will take to quite hard pruning in early summer, as will bay trees.

Herb hedges

By cutting herbs into hedge shapes you stop them from flowering. In the case of rosemary and lavender I think this a shame, but I have to admit that the sight of box and cotton lavender with no flowers, clipped and shaped in the parterre garden at Ham House, on the outskirts of London, is very pleasing to the eye. On a small scale though, I feel you do need cotton lavender flowers.

Hedges can be straight edged, for example with cotton lavender, obelisk or barrel shaped, which suits wall germander, or round, which is appropriate for curry plants. Box can be pruned from early summer onwards and produces very tight growth, making it an ideal subject for topiary and shaped hedges.

Mulching and feeding

Mulching is a way of enriching and insulating the soil around your herb plants. Although herbs can suffer from too much moisture in areas where the soil dries out very quickly it helps, in the height of summer, to retain some water and protect the roots from burning.

Mulch can be well-rotted leaf-mould, forest bark or peat. Herbs respond best to the organic leaf-mould mulch, which can be applied lightly at first and then built up into the winter months. I like to place the leaves of comfrey about the soil and allow the natural decomposition and the work of earthworms to incorporate it into the beds. Both comfrey and yarrow are good compost activators.

Do not use a mulch on compacted clay soils. In any case, you should have dug in plenty of grit, sharp sand and well-rotted manure well before planting, and an addition of part or all of these materials can help each season. Lawn clippings are often used but should be left for a week or two and turned regularly, otherwise they are too 'hot' and also have a tendency to mat together. In the spring you need to remove as much mulch as possible to allow light and air to all of the plant, and to avoid it becoming too wet.

With the soil enriched, you can start feeding once winter has passed; feed with soluble feeds about every two weeks, gradually increasing the amount as the growing season gets going.

If you have prepared your soil well, then you will find you need very little feed, and, as I always advocate, you will not pamper your herbs too much. Although parsley, basil and some salad herbs green up well with feeding, you do not want your herbs growing too fast and becoming soft and leggy which generous feeding promotes.

Pest control

Long before the introduction of chemical pesticides, people discovered the use of aromatic and bitter herbs to repel insects and vermin. In Morocco they would surround their orchards with hedges of rosemary. If you are troubled by ants then pennyroyal will deter them. I have sprinkled the leaves of pennyroyal along a windowsill, where ants were coming into the kitchen, and it was extremely effective, driving them all away immediately.

There are a number of pest repellent herbs. Traditional ones are tansy, feverfew, fleabane and elecampane (*Inula helenium*). The strong odour of garlic and other alliums repel carrot fly and offer protection to roses. A number of aromatic herbs, such as rosemary, thyme, winter savory, hyssop and marjoram, deter cabbage moth and other beetles. Mint is another herb which protects the cabbage family and deters flea beetle. Brought into the home it helps to keep flies out of the house as well. Rue and wormwood are the strongest smelling and most pungent of all the insect repellents.

All of these herbs can be made into infusions with which to spray your plants. Instead of throwing the used herbs away you can spread them about among the plants as a light mulch. Soap flakes can be added to the mixture to help kill aphids, trapping them and suffocating them. As a rule of thumb fresh herbs can be used in measures of one handful to 600ml/1 pint of water.

I made up a garlic spray to control insect pests some years ago. I crushed 20 cloves of garlic and added a little paraffin oil. Making a pure soap solution in 300ml/½ pint of hot water, I poured this over the garlic and left it for a day before warming it up again and straining it. After boiling it I used a ratio of 1:100 parts with water. It seemed to

be very effective. But everywhere I used it, afterwards stank of garlic, and when the sun caused the cork to eject like a bullet in the shed one day, it was several days before we could bear to go in there! Effective as it was I have given this one up in favour of more sweet-smelling infusions such as southernwood.

If you are plagued by insects at night in your garden, then gather a few aromatic herbs – sage, rosemary, southernwood, rue – and place them in a can or on a deep tray and ignite them with dried grass or paper. This helps to smoke them out and sweetens the air. I have used this method on a spent barbecue.

The comforting thing about all these sprays and deterrents is that they are all safe, and offer no harm to bees and other garden 'friends'. If you are lucky enough to have a toad to eat the slugs and snails, and, as we once had, a friendly neighbourhood fox that killed off the rats and mice, then you should feel very well protected.

Above: Low growing thymes thrive happily in gravel and will soon grow into one another to form an attractive garden feature.

Right: Alternatively an old stone sink is a good way to show off low-growing herbs such as thymes.

PROPAGATION CHART

HERB	PROPAGATION	LATE WINTER	SPRING	SUMMER	AUTUMN	EARLY WINTER
Alpine Strawberry	Divide runners		✓			
Basil	Sow seed		✓ HEAT	✓		
Bay	Take cuttings				✓	
Chives	Sow seed divide bulblets	✓ D	✓ D	✓		
Coriander	Sow seed		✓	✓		
Dill	Sow seed		✓ HEAT	✓		
Fennel	Sow seed or divide offsets		✓ HEAT	✓		
Lavender	Take cuttings Sow seed		✓		✓ C	
Marjoram	Divide roots cuttings		✓ D	✓ D	✓ C	

PROPAGATION CHART

KEY		
C Cuttings	D Root Division	HEAT Heated greenhouse

HERB	PROPAGATION	LATE WINTER	SPRING	SUMMER	AUTUMN	EARLY WINTER
Mint	Divide roots cuttings	✓ D	✓ D	✓ C		
Parsley	Sow seed	✓	✓	✓	✓	✓
Rosemary	Take cuttings		✓	✓	✓	
Savory (summer)	Sow seed		✓			
Savory (winter)	Cuttings		✓ D/C	✓	✓ D	
Sage	Divide roots cuttings		✓	✓ C		
Sorrel	Divide roots sow seed		✓ D	✓		
Thyme	Divide roots cuttings sow seed	✓	✓	✓	✓	
Woodruff	Divide roots			✓		

Text on chalkboard in image:
CORIANDER, DILL,
PARSLEY 1.10
COWSLIPS + PRIMROSE 1.00
OTHER SMALL 1.20
HERBS
MYRTLE 2.95/BA
PRIMULA 2.00   4.50

Useful Addresses

Associations and Societies

British Herbal Medicine Association
Lane House
Cowling
Keighley
West Yorkshire BD22 0LX

British Herb Society
134 Buckingham Palace Road
London SW1W 9SA

British Herb Trade Association
NFU Building
22 Long Acre
Covent Garden
London WC2E 9LY

Chelsea Physic Garden
Friends of the Chelsea Physic Garden
66 Royal Hospital Road
London SW3 4HS

Henry Doubleday Association
Ryton Gardens
Ryton-on-Dunsmore
Coventry CV8 3LG

National Institute of Medical Herbalists
148 Forest Road
Tunbridge Wells
Kent TN2 5EY

The Soil Association
86 Colston Street
Bristol BS1 5BB

The Tradescant Trust
Friends of the Museum of Garden History
Lambeth Palace Road
London SE1 7LB

Herb Nurseries

Cheshire Herbs
Fourfields
Forest Road
Little Budworth
near Tarporley
Cheshire CW6 9ES

Hollington Nurseries
Woolton Hill
Newbury
Berkshire RG15 9XT

Langley Boxwood Nursery
National Collection - Buxus
Rake
near Liss
Hampshire GU33 7JL

Jekka's Herb Farm
Rose Cottage
Shellards Lane
Alveston
Bristol BS12 2SY

Norfolk LavenderCaley Mill
Heacham
KIngs Lynn
Norfolk PE31 7JE

Dried Herbs and Herb Products

Hambledon Herbs
Court Farm
Milverton
Somerset TA4 1NF

Neal's Yard Remedies
14-15 Neal's Yard
Covent Garden
London WC2 9DP

Index